ISBN 978-0-656-86023-4
PIBN 11112314

Historic, archived document

Do not assume content reflects current
scientific knowledge, policies, or practices.

₩/STA

**United States
Department of
Agriculture**

Forest
Service

North Central
Forest Experiment
Station

Resource
Bulletin **NC-77**

Primary Forest Products Industry and Timber Use, Kansas, 1980

James E. Blyth, Leonard K. Gould, and W. Brad Smith

FOREWORD

This Bulletin contains the results of a detailed study of forest industry, timber products output from roundwood, and associated primary mill wood and bark residue in Kansas in 1980. Such detailed information is necessary for intelligent planning and decisionmaking in wood procurement, forest resource management, and forest industry development. Likewise, researchers need current forest industry and timber products output information to plan projects.

Special thanks are given to the primary wood-using firms that supplied information for this study. Their cooperation is greatly appreciated.

Quantities shown may vary slightly from one table to another because of rounding differences, but these differences are insignificant.

CONTENTS

North Central Forest Experiment Station
Forest Service—U.S. Department of Agriculture
1992 Folwell Avenue
St. Paul, Minnesota 55108
Manuscript approved for publication March 16, 1984
September 1984

PRIMARY FOREST PRODUCTS INDUSTRY AND TIMBER USE, KANSAS, 1980

James E. Blyth, *Principal Market Analyst,*
St. Paul, Minnesota,
Leonard K. Gould, *Extension Forester,*
Utilization and Marketing,
Manhattan, Kansas,
and **W. Brad Smith,** *Mensurationist,*
St. Paul, Minnesota

HIGHLIGHTS

- The number of active primary wood-using mills declined from 95 in 1964 to 63 in 1980. All of the net loss in mills was in the two eastern Forest Survey Units (fig. 1). In the Western Unit, active mills rose from 8 to 14.
- Timber products output (TPO) from roundwood climbed 182 percent between 1964 and 1980 to 23.3 million cubic feet. Major harvest gains were in white oak, red oak, ash, hackberry, and cottonwood. These species, along with walnut, were the principal species harvested and provided 70 percent of the roundwood cut in 1980.
- Average annual lumber production at sawmills increased. Between 1964 and 1980, the number of medium-size sawmills rose from 6 to 11 while the number of small sawmills dropped from 73 to 48.
- Loggers harvested more than 10 million cubic feet of timber products in each of the two eastern Units, accounting for 87 percent of the State's roundwood harvest.
- Estimated fuelwood production from roundwood was 255,000 cords and constituted 77 percent of the TPO from roundwood. Fuelwood production from roundwood in 1980 was 3.75 times greater than fuelwood cut in 1964.
- Saw log production in 1980 was 31.9 million board feet, nearly double the output in 1964 and 39 percent above 1969 production. Demand for oak grew rapidly since 1969. Leading species cut were walnut and cottonwood.
- Elm losses to Dutch Elm disease during the 1970's led to a 53 percent drop in elm saw log production between 1969 and 1980.
- Most of the saw log production is processed in Kansas. Only 1.4 million board feet was exported, primarily to Missouri. The Southeastern Unit led in production (16.8 million board feet).

- Counties each producing more than 1 million board feet of saw logs were (in order of importance) Neosho, Labette, Allen, Woodson, Douglas, Bourbon, Shawnee, Montgomery, Franklin, and Leavenworth. These counties provided 49 percent of the Kansas saw log harvest.
- Five counties—Douglas, Franklin, Jefferson, Miami, and Linn—each cut more than 0.5 million board feet of walnut saw logs.
- Kansas sawmills received 35.6 million board feet of logs in 1980. Missouri supplied 3.2 million board feet and another 1.9 million board feet was supplied in nearly equal divisions from Nebraska, Oklahoma, and Iowa. Kansas sawmills imported more than one-third (36 percent) of their walnut log requirements in 1980.
- Sawmills in the Northeastern Unit received 52 percent of the total saw log receipts in Kansas. Northeastern Unit sawmills sawed more than 90 percent of the walnut saw logs received by Kansas mills.
- Ninety percent of the imported saw log volume (including all of the imported walnut) was shipped to Northeastern Unit mills.
- An estimated 350,000 posts were cut in Kansas, about 64 percent of the 1964 level. Osage orange was the preferred species.
- During 1980 on a green weight basis, Kansas primary wood-using mills generated 47,000 tons of coarse (chippable) wood residue, 28,000 tons of fine wood residue, and 20,000 tons of bark. Fuel was the dominant use for bark; 42 percent of the bark was not used for any purpose.
- Great progress has been made since 1964 in finding uses for wood residue generated at primary wood-using mills. Seventy-six percent of the coarse residue was used in 1980 compared with 19 percent in 1964. Three-fourths of the fine residue was used

KANSAS

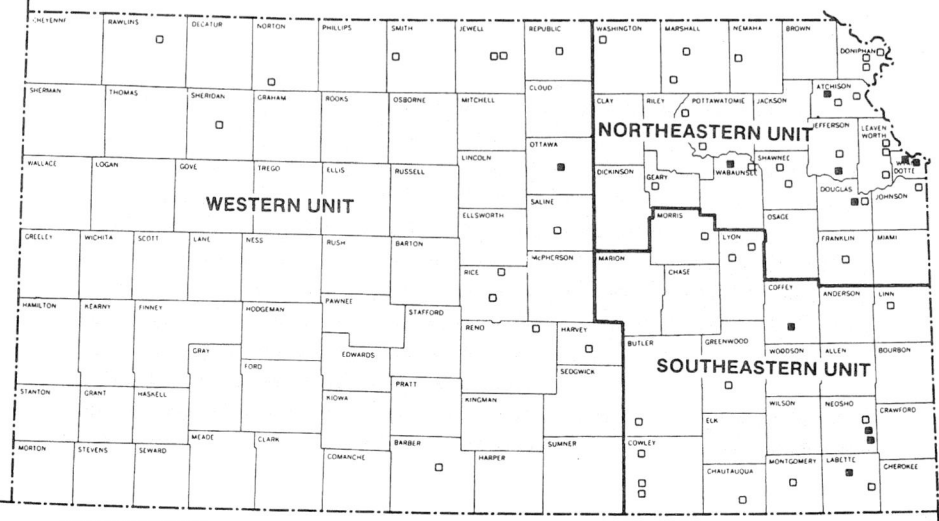

■ MEDIUM SAWMILL
□ SMALL SAWMILL

Figure 1.—*Active sawmills and Forest Survey Units in Kansas, 1980. Sawmills are classed by volume of lumber produced in 1980: medium = 1 to 5 million board feet; small = less than 1 million board feet. Forest Survey Units are the geographic areas used by the Forest Inventory and Analysis Project to report periodic inventories and use of the Nations's forest resources.*

in 1980, up from 48 percent in 1964. Chief uses for coarse residue were for fuel and fiber products. Major uses for fine residue were as fuel, poultry litter, livestock bedding, mulch, etc.

APPENDIX

STUDY METHODS

Except for fuelwood and posts, data for this publication came from canvassing with a formal questionnaire all of the known primary wood-using mills that use Kansas logs and bolts. All canvassing in Kansas was initially done by mail by the Kansas Cooperative Extension Service, State and Extension Forestry (KCES); follow-up on nonrespondents was by mail, telephone, and personal contact. For a few Kansas mills that did not furnish complete data, KCES utilization and marketing specialists provided estimates based on prior knowledge and contacts. Similar cooperative studies in other North Central States by the

North Central Forest Experiment Station and State forest agencies provided data from out-of-State mills that used Kansas logs and bolts.

General offices of railroads serving Kansas were solicited by the Station to determine the volume of veneer logs shipped from points in Kansas to seaports for export overseas.

Estimates of 1980 fuelwood and post production in Kansas were made by the KCES based on recent production studies, records, and discussions with others knowledgeable about these products.

The Station edited and compiled the data.

SAMPLING ERROR

Because all primary wood-using mills were canvassed, there is no sampling error for the roundwood products they use.

DEFINITION OF TERMS

Roundwood.—Logs, bolts, or other round sections cut from trees (including chips from roundwood).

Timber products output from roundwood.—Logs and bolts (including chips from roundwood) harvested for saw logs, veneer logs, cooperage logs, pulpwood, posts, fuelwood, and other products.

Forest Survey Unit.— A geographical area (group of counties) used by the Forest Inventory and Analysis Project to report periodic inventories and use of the Nation's forest resources.

Primary wood-using mills.—Mills using roundwood products (including chips from roundwood).

Primary wood-using mill residue.—Wood materials (coarse and fine) and bark not utilized for principal products at mills using roundwood. These residues include wood products (byproducts) obtained incidental to production of principal products and wood materials not utilized for some product.

Coarse mill residue.—Wood residue suitable for chipping such as slabs, edgings, and veneer cores.

Fine mill residue.—Wood residue not suitable for chipping such as sawdust and veneer clippings.

COMMON AND SCIENTIFIC NAMES OF TREE SPECIES IN KANSAS

SOFTWOODS
Redcedar (eastern) .... *Juniperus virginiana*
HARDWOODS
Ash (green) .... *Fraxinus pennsylvanica*
Basswood(American) .... *Tilia americana*
Birch (river) .... *Betula nigra*
Boxelder .... *Acer negundo*
Cherry (black) .... *Prunus serotina*
Catalpa (northern) .... *Catalpa speciosa*
Cottonwood(eastern) .... *Populus deltoides*
Elm
    American elm .... *Ulmus americana*

Rock elm .... *Ulmus thomasii*
Siberian elm .... *Ulmus pumila*
Slippery elm .... *Ulmus rubra*
Hackberry .... *Celtis occidentalis*
Hickory
    Bitternut hickory .... *Carya cordiformis*
    Mockernut hickory .... *Carya tomentosa*
    Pecan .... *Carya illinoensis*
    Pignut hickory .... *Carya glabra*
    Shagbark hickory .... *Carya ovata*
    Shellbark hickory .... *Carya laciniosa*
Honeylocust .... *Gleditsia triacanthos*
Kentucky coffeetree .... *Gymnocladus dioicus*
Locust (black) .... *Robinia pseudoacacia*
Maple
    Hard maple
        Black maple .... *Acer nigrum*
        Sugar maple .... *Acer saccharum*
    Soft maple
        Red maple .... *Acer rubrum* var. *rubrum*
        Silver maple .... *Acer saccharinum*
Mulberry
    Red mulberry .... *Morus rubra*
    White mulberry .... *Morus alba*
Oak
    Select red oaks
        Northern red oak .... *Quercus rubra*
        Shumard oak .... *Quercus shumardii*
    Other red oaks
        Black oak .... *Quercus velutina*
        Pin oak .... *Quercus palustris*
        Shingle oak .... *Quercus imbricaria*
    Select white oaks
        Bur oak .... *Quercus macrocarpa*
        Chinkapin oak .... *Quercus muehlenbergii*
        White oak .... *Quercus alba*
    Other white oaks
        Post oak .... *Quercus stellata* var. *stellata*
Persimmon (common) ...... *Diospyros virginiana*
Sycamore (American) .... *Platanus occidentalis*
Walnut (Black) .... *Juglans nigra*
Willow (black) .... *Salix nigra*

Table 1.--Timber products output from roundwood by species and product Kansas, 1980

Species	All products MCF[1]	Saw logs MBF[2]	Saw logs MCF[1]	Fuelwood Cords[3]	Fuelwood MCF[1]	Posts M pieces[4]	Posts MCF[1]	Veneer logs MBF[2]	Veneer logs MCF[1]	Cooperage logs MBF[2]	Cooperage logs MCF[1]
Softwoods											
Eastern redcedar	92	321	66	--	--	35	26	--	--	--	--
Total	92	321	66	--	--	35	26	--	--	--	--
Hardwoods											
Ash	2,685	2,183	367	33,150	2,318	--	--	--	--	--	--
Basswood	18	10	1	250	17	--	--	--	--	--	--
Birch	9	58	9	-	-	-	-	--	--	--	--
Black cherry	3	18	3	-	-	-	-	--	--	--	--
Cottonwood	1,832	6,107	940	12,750	892	--	--	--	--	--	--
Elm	1,116	1,458	222	12,750	894	--	--	--	--	--	--
Hackberry	1,931	3,193	504	20,400	1,427	--	--	--	--	--	--
Pecan	57	348	57	--	--	--	--	--	--	--	--
Other hickory	545	74	11	7,650	534	--	--	--	--	--	--
Hard maple	25	--	--	90	25	--	--	--	--	--	--
Soft maple	779	1,543	246	7,650	533	--	--	--	--	--	--
Red oak	3,645	2,931	521	44,427	3,111	27	13	--	--	--	--
White oak	4,669	3,225	569	57,573	4,030	26	14	59	12	264	44
Sycamore	397	1,417	218	2,550	179	--	--	--	--	--	--
Walnut	1,609	8,955	1,362	2,550	178	--	--	478	69	--	--
Osage-orange	796	--	--	9,500	665	227	131	--	--	--	--
Other hardwoods	3,065	45	6	43,400	3,040	35	19	--	--	--	--
Total	23,181	31,565	5,036	255,000	17,843	315	177	537	81	264	44
All species	23,273	31,886	5,102	255,000	17,843	350	203	537	81	264	44

1/Thousand cubic feet.
2/Thousand board feet, International 1/4-inch rule.
3/Standard cords.
4/Thousand pieces.

Table 2.--Timber products output from roundwood by
species, Kansas, 1964 and 1980

(In thousand cubic feet)

Species	1964	1980	Change
Softwoods			
Eastern redcedar	27	92	65
Total	27	92	65
Hardwoods			
Ash	770	2,685	1,915
Basswood	3	18	15
Black cherry	--	3	3
Cottonwood	517	1,832	1,315
Elm	376	1,116	740
Hackberry	345	1,931	1,586
Pecan	--	57	57
Other hickory	1060	545	-515
Hard maple	--	25	25
Soft maple	987	779	-208
Red oak	869	3,645	2,776
White oak	1,882	4,669	2,787
Sycamore	130	397	267
Walnut	1,112	1,609	497
Other hardwoods	169	3,870	3,701
Total	8,220	23,181	14,961
All species	8,247	23,273	15,026

Table 3.--Number of active primary wood-using mills by Unit, Kansas, 1964 and 1980

Kind of mill	All Units		Northeastern		Southeastern		Western	
	1964	1980	1964	1980	1964	1980	1964	1980
Sawmills								
Small[1]/	73	48	35	22	31	13	7	13
Medium[2]/	6	11	4	6	2	4	--	1
Cooperage mills	10	1	3	1	6	--	1	--
Charcoal plants	1	--	--	--	1	--	--	--
Miscellaneous plants[3]/	5	3	1	--	4	3	--	--
Total	95	63	43	29	44	20	8	14

[1]/Annual lumber output less than 1 million board feet.

[2]/Annual lumber output from 1 to 5 million board feet.

[3]/Fence post concentration yards and treating plants.

Table 4.--Timber products output from roundwood by species
and Unit, Kansas, 1980

(In thousand cubic feet)

Species	All Units	Northeastern Unit	Southeastern Unit	Western Unit
Softwoods				
Eastern redcedar	92	44	13	35
Total	92	44	13	35
Hardwoods				
Ash	2,685	715	1,478	492
Basswood	18	18	--	--
Birch	9	9	--	--
Black cherry	3	3	--	--
Cottonwood	1,832	779	543	510
Elm	1,116	491	501	124
Hackberry	1,931	756	984	191
Pecan	57	--	57	--
Other hickory	545	349	196	--
Hard maple	25	--	25	--
Soft maple	779	372	403	4
Red oak	3,645	1,841	1,783	21
White oak	4,669	2,100	1,904	665
Sycamore	397	95	290	12
Walnut	1,609	977	616	16
Osage-orange	796	159	279	358
Other hardwoods	3,065	1,336	1,112	617
Total	23,181	10,000	10,171	3,010
All species	23,273	10,044	10,184	3,045

Table 5.--Saw log production by species,
Kansas, 1969 and 1980

(In thousand board feet)$^{1/}$

Species	1969	1980	Change
Softwoods			
Eastern redcedar	--	321	321
Total	--	321	321
Hardwoods			
Ash	1,396	2,183	787
Basswood	70	10	-60
Birch	80	58	-22
Black cherry	25	18	-7
Cottonwood	6,108	6,107	-1
Elm	3,108	1,458	-1,650
Hackberry	2,990	3,193	203
Pecan	309	348	39
Other hickory	65	74	9
Hard maple	25	--	-25
Soft maple	1,216	1,543	327
Red oak	1,117	2,931	1,814
White oak	894	3,225	2,331
Sycamore	1,303	1,417	114
Walnut	4,150	8,955	4,805
Other hardwoods	71	45	-26
Total	22,927	31,565	8,638
All species	22,927	31,886	8,959

$^{1/}$International 1/4-inch rule.

6

Table 6.--Saw log production by Unit, species, and
State of destination, Kansas, 1980

(In thousand board feet)[1]

ALL UNITS

Species	All States	State of destination		
		Kansas	Missouri	Nebraska
Softwoods				
Eastern redcedar	321	321	--	--
Total	321	321	--	--
Hardwoods				
Ash	2,183	2,175	8	
Basswood	10	9	1	
Birch	58	55	3	--
Black cherry	18	18	--	--
Cottonwood	6,107	6,042	61	4
Elm	1,458	1,455	3	--
Hackberry	3,193	3,193	--	
Pecan	348	347	1	
Other hickory	74	68	6	
Soft maple	1,543	1,538	5	--
Red oak	2,931	2,637	294	--
White oak	3,225	3,054	46	125
Sycamore	1,417	1,387	30	--
Walnut	8,955	8,161	776	18
Other hardwoods	45	45	--	--
Total	31,565	30,184	1,234	147
All species	31,886	30,505	1,234	147

NORTHEASTERN UNIT

Species	All States	Kansas	Missouri	Nebraska
Softwoods				
Eastern redcedar	128	128	--	--
Total	128	128	--	--
Hardwoods				
Ash	694	691	3	
Basswood	10	9	1	
Birch	55	55	--	--
Black cherry	18	18	--	
Cottonwood	2,382	2,347	35	
Elm	419	416	3	
Hackberry	829	829	--	
Pecan	4	3	1	
Other hickory	69	68	1	
Soft maple	280	280	--	--
Red oak	1,027	992	35	--
White oak	1,223	1,082	17	124
Sycamore	226	216	10	--
Walnut	5,287	4,758	511	18
Other hardwoods	4	4	--	--
Total	12,527	11,768	617	142
All species	12,655	11,896	617	142

(Table 6 continued on next page)

[1] International 1/4-inch rule.

(Table 6 continued)

	All	State of destination		
Species	States	Kansas	Missouri	Nebraska
SOUTHEASTERN UNIT				
Softwoods				
Eastern redcedar	25	25	--	--
Total	25	25	--	--
Hardwoods				
Ash	1,310	1,305	5	
Basswood	--	--	--	
Birch	3	--	3	
Black cherry	--	--	--	
Cottonwood	2,846	2,820	26	
Elm	955	955	--	--
Hackberry	2,120	2,120	--	--
Pecan	343	343	--	--
Other hickory	5	--	5	--
Soft maple	1,263	1,258	5	
Red oak	1,783	1,524	259	
White oak	1,452	1,423	29	--
Sycamore	1,117	1,097	20	
Walnut	3,551	3,286	265	--
Other hardwoods	34	34	--	--
Total	16,782	16,165	617	--
All species	16,807	16,190	617	--
WESTERN UNIT				
Softwoods				
Eastern redcedar	168	168	--	--
Total	168	168	--	--
Hardwoods				
Ash	179	179		
Basswood	--	--		
Birch	--	--		--
Black cherry	--	--		--
Cottonwood	879	875		4
Elm	84	84		--
Hackberry	244	244		
Pecan	1	1		
Other hickory	--	--		
Soft maple	--	--	--	--
Red oak	121	121		--
White oak	550	549	--	1
Sycamore	74	74		--
Walnut	117	117	--	--
Other hardwoods	7	7	--	--
Total	2,256	2,251	--	5
All species	2,424	2,419	--	5

8

Table 7.--Saw log production by Unit, county, and species, Kansas, 1980

(In thousand board feet)[1]

NORTHEASTERN UNIT

County	All species	Eastern redcedar	Ash	Cotton-wood	Elm	Hack-berry	Pecan	Other hickory	Soft maple	Red oak	White oak	Syca-more	Walnut	Other hardwoods
Atchison	628	1	55	19	10	43	3	1	26	34	54	7	371	4
Brown	114	--	21	6	--	12	--	--	10	3	8	--	54	--
Clay	238	--	33	35	21	46	--	--	--	--	68	14	21	--
Dickinson	35	--	--	--	--	--	--	--	--	--	--	--	35	--
Doniphan	743	3	15	159	24	36	--	--	--	46	22	17	416	5
Douglas	1,357	49	91	103	49	112	--	--	42	196	77	29	605	4
Franklin	1,076	--	52	76	40	61	--	22	31	175	49	26	537	7
Geary	168	8	4	35	7	14	--	--	--	--	28	--	72	--
Jackson	281	1	45	19	1	29	--	--	21	10	23	3	129	--
Jefferson	996	1	116	25	22	76	--	--	49	32	35	--	640	--
Johnson	579	--	11	12	29	43	--	6	7	133	41	8	285	4
Leavenworth	1,070	7	58	78	59	104	--	17	7	152	68	30	487	3
Marshall	722	12	62	57	25	64	--	--	19	40	208	3	232	--
Miami	843	--	24	25	24	14	1	22	28	115	38	31	520	1
Nemaha	270	7	25	28	14	36	--	--	11	17	51	1	25	55
Osage	541	--	21	179	21	0	--	--	7	6	30	7	270	--
Pottawatomie	736	5	21	385	10	29	--	--	--	7	123	14	142	--
Riley	367	21	7	222	--	3	--	--	--	--	60	--	54	--
Shawnee	1,140	8	13	495	63	76	--	1	22	57	113	36	253	3
Wabaunsee	604	5	--	417	--	2	--	--	--	4	74	--	102	--
Washington	117	--	20	7	--	29	--	--	--	--	53	--	7	1
Wyandotte	30	--	--	--	--	--	--	--	--	--	--	--	30	--
Total	12,655	128	694	2,382	419	829	4	69	280	1,027	1,223	226	5,287	87

SOUTHEASTERN UNIT

County	All species	Eastern redcedar	Ash	Cotton-wood	Elm	Hack-berry	Pecan	Other hickory	Soft maple	Red oak	White oak	Syca-more	Walnut	Other hardwoods
Allen	1,902	--	138	276	138	483	--	--	97	273	207	131	159	--
Anderson	337	--	--	7	21	--	--	--	35	7	--	21	246	--
Bourbon	1,315	--	138	16	21	21	30	5	165	256	96	79	488	--
Butler	397	1	17	129	35	55	--	--	--	28	79	8	45	--
Chase	124	--	21	14	7	14	--	--	--	--	28	--	40	--
Chautauqua	260	--	--	4	3	7	1	--	--	25	21	8	191	--
Cherokee	804	--	122	37	54	37	52	--	123	32	52	53	239	3
Coffey	437	--	34	70	32	42	--	--	29	28	18	21	142	21
Cowley	354	5	14	139	18	29	12	--	1	11	32	14	67	12
Crawford	643	1	48	61	38	29	26	--	36	106	43	35	220	--
Elk	39	--	--	--	--	--	--	--	--	--	--	--	39	--
Greenwood	270	1	8	15	6	50	--	--	12	39	37	22	80	--
Labette	2,121	3	127	453	181	383	56	--	179	338	131	102	168	--
Linn	709	1	--	15	--	--	--	--	--	90	14	18	570	1
Lyon	625	7	50	114	34	51	--	--	43	40	117	56	113	--
Marion	39	--	--	--	--	--	--	--	--	--	--	--	39	--
Montgomery	1,120	--	70	133	139	157	98	--	37	86	93	95	212	--
Morris	307	3	48	62	8	39	1	--	--	--	77	21	48	--
Neosho	2,751	3	340	418	170	444	42	--	355	245	252	290	192	--
Wilson	638	--	54	35	40	62	25	--	62	95	48	57	160	--
Woodson	1,615	--	81	848	10	217	--	--	89	84	107	86	93	--
Total	16,807	25	1,310	2,846	955	2,120	343	5	1,263	1,783	1,452	1,117	3,551	37

(Table 7 continued on next page)

[1] International 1/4-inch rule.

9

(Table 7 continued)

WESTERN UNIT

County	All species	Eastern redcedar	Ash	Cotton-wood	Elm	Hack-berry	Pecan	Other hickory	Soft maple	Red oak	White oak	Syca-more	Walnut	Other hardwoods
Barber	145	145	--	--	--	--	--	--	--	--	--	--	--	--
Barton	106	--	--	83	--	--	--	--	--	--	--	--	--	--
Cloud	467	7	39	131	--	58	--	--	--	41	17	6	14	--
Deca urt	34	--	28	3	21	--	--	--	--	--	156	21	3	--
Harvey	194	3	7	48	--	35	--	--	--	14	--	--	21	--
Jewell	42	--	--	7	--	1	--	--	--	3	48	--	3	--
Kingman	15	--	--	15	14	--	--	--	--	--	25	--	--	--
Lincoln	77	--	--	14	--	21	--	--	--	--	--	--	--	--
Mcpherson	1	--	--	--	--	--	--	--	--	--	28	--	1	--
Norton	15	1	7	4	--	--	--	--	--	--	--	--	3	--
O awat	497	7	48	97	41	62	--	--	--	48	124	35	35	--
Rawlins	22	--	17	--	4	--	--	--	--	7	--	--	1	--
Reno	109	1	14	55	--	7	--	--	--	7	25	--	1	--
Republic	136	1	19	25	3	33	--	--	--	--	48	--	3	--
Rice	174	--	--	118	--	6	--	--	--	--	36	11	--	--
Saline	62	--	--	21	--	11	--	--	--	--	30	--	--	--
Sheridan	75	--	--	72	--	--	--	--	--	--	--	--	3	--
Smi ht	33	--	--	10	1	4	--	--	--	1	13	--	3	--
Sumner	220	4	--	176	--	6	1	--	--	--	--	1	26	1
Total	2,424	168	179	879	84	244	1	--	--	121	550	74	117	7
State total	31,886	321	2,183	6,107	1,458	3,193	348	74	1,543	2,931	3,225	1,417	8,955	131

Table 8.--Saw log receipts in Kansas by Unit, species and State of origin, 1980

(In thousand board feet)[1/]

ALL UNITS

Species	All States	State of origin				
		Kansas	Missouri	Nebraska	Oklahoma	Iowa
Softwoods						
Eastern redcedar	321	321	--	--	--	--
Total	321	321	--	--	--	--
Hardwoods						
Ash	2,175	2,175	--	--	--	--
Basswood	9	9	--	--	--	--
Birch	55	55	--	--	--	--
Black cherry	18	18	--	--	--	--
Cottonwood	6,154	6,042	32	80	--	--
Elm	1,541	1,455	--	--	86	--
Hackberry	3,233	3,193	13	3	24	--
Pecan	399	347	11	--	41	--
Other hickory	68	68	--	--	--	--
Soft maple	1,626	1,538	88	--	--	--
Red oak	2,713	2,637	76	--	--	--
White oak	3,114	3,054	23	--	37	--
Sycamore	1,387	1,387	--	--	--	--
Walnut	12,716	8,161	2,967	587	414	587
Other hardwoods	45	45	--	--	--	--
Total	35,253	30,184	3,210	670	602	587
All species	35,574	30,505	3,210	670	602	587
NORTHEASTERN UNIT						
Softwoods						
Eastern redcedar	124	124	--	--	--	--
Total	124	124	--	--	--	--
Hardwoods						
Ash	693	693	--	--	--	--
Basswood	9	9	--	--	--	--
Birch	55	55	--	--	--	--
Black cherry	18	18	--	--	--	--
Cottonwood	2,199	2,167	32	--	--	--
Elm	360	360	--	--	--	--
Hackberry	826	826	--	--	--	--
Pecan	3	3	--	--	--	--
Other hickory	68	68	--	--	--	--
Soft maple	252	252	--	--	--	--
Red oak	964	958	6	--	--	--
White oak	995	995	--	--	--	--
Sycamore	167	167	--	--	--	--
Walnut	11,864	7,309	2,967	587	414	587
Other hardwoods	4	4	--	--	--	--
Total	18,477	13,884	3,005	587	414	587
All species	18,601	14,008	3,005	587	414	587

(Table 8 continued on next page)

[1/] International 1/4-inch rule.

11

(Table 8 continued)

SOUTHEASTERN UNIT

Species	All States	State of origin				
		Kansas	Missouri	Nebraska	Oklahoma	Iowa
Softwoods						
Eastern redcedar	33	33	--	--	--	--
Total	33	33	--	--	--	--
hardwoods						
Ash	1,312	1,312			--	
Cottonwood	3,101	3,101	--		--	
Elm	1,048	962	--		86	
Hackberry	2,136	2,099	13		24	
Pecan	396	344	11		41	
Soft maple	1,374	1,286	88		--	
Red oak	1,607	1,537	70		--	
White oak	1,456	1,396	23		37	
Sycamore	1,133	1,133	--	--	--	
Walnut	699	699	--	--	--	--
Other hardwoods	40	40	--	--	--	--
Total	14,302	13,909	205	--	188	--
All species	14,335	13,942	205	--	188	--

WESTERN UNIT

Species	All States	State of origin				
		Kansas	Missouri	Nebraska	Oklahoma	Iowa
Softwoods						
Eastern redcedar	164	164	--	--	--	--
Total	164	164	--	--	--	--
Hardwoods						
Ash	170	170		--		
Cottonwood	854	774		80		
Elm	133	133		--		
Hackberry	271	268		3		
Red oak	142	142		--		
White oak	663	663				
Sycamore	87	87				
Walnut	153	153	--	--	--	--
Other hardwoods	1	1	--	--	--	--
Total	2,474	2,391	--	83	--	--
All species	2,638	2,555	--	83	--	--

Table 9.--Residue produced at primary wood-using mills by type of material, type of use, and Unit, Kansas, 1980

(In thousand tons green weight)

Unit and type of use	Wood residue						Bark	
	Total		Coarse[1]		Fine[2]			
	Softwood	Hardwood	Softwood	Hardwood	Softwood	Hardwood	Softwood	Hardwood
Northeastern Unit								
Industrial fuel	--	18.84	--	12.03	--	6.81	--	5.11
Domestic fuel[3]	0.14	9.53	0.14	9.41	--	0.12	0.02	3.97
Miscellaneous[3]	.07	4.67	--	--	.07	4.67	--	--
Not used	.01	6.15	.01	3.34	--	2.81	--	1.42
Total	.22	39.19	.15	24.78	.07	14.41	.02	10.50
Southeastern Unit								
Fiber products	--	8.32	--	8.32	--	--	--	--
Charcoal	--	.31	--	.28	--	.03	--	.12
Industrial fuel	--	.07	--	.07	--	--	--	.03
Domestic fuel[3]	.03	3.07	.03	2.96	--	.11	--	1.17
Miscellaneous[3]	.01	7.42	--	.03	.01	7.39	--	.02
Not used	--	11.35	--	7.57	--	3.78	--	6.59
Total	.04	30.54	.03	19.23	.01	11.31	--	7.93
Western Unit								
Domestic fuel[3]	.13	3.51	.12	2.62	.01	.89	.02	1.07
Miscellaneous[3]	.06	.68	--	.05	.06	.63	--	--
Not used	.16	1.06	.10	.64	.06	.42	.02	.34
Total	.35	5.25	.22	3.31	.13	1.94	.04	1.41
All Units								
Fiber products	--	8.32	--	8.32	--	--	--	--
Charcoal	--	.31	--	.28	--	.03	--	.12
Industrial fuel	--	18.91	-	12.10	--	6.81	--	5.14
Domestic fuel[3]	.30	16.11	.29	14.99	.01	1.12	.04	6.21
Miscellaneous[3]	.14	12.77	--	.08	.14	12.69	--	.02
Not used	.17	18.56	.11	11.55	.06	7.01	.02	8.35
Total	.61	74.98	.40	47.32	.21	27.66	.06	19.84

[1] Suitable for chipping such as slabs, edgings, veneer cores, etc.
[2] Not suitable for chipping such as sawdust, veneer clippings, etc.
[3] Livestock bedding, poultry litter, mulch, small dimension, specialty items, etc.

Blyth, James E.; Gould, Leonard K.; Smith, W. Brad.
  Primary forest products industry and timber use, Kansas, 1980. Resour.
  Bull. NC-77. St. Paul, MN: U.S. Department of Agriculture, Forest
  Service, North Central Forest Experiment Station; 1984. 13 p.

  Highlights recent Kansas forest industry trends, production and
  receipts of saw logs in 1980, and production of other timber products
  in 1980. Reports on wood and bark residue generated at primary mills
  and the disposition of this residue.

KEY WORDS: Saw logs, sawmills, fuelwood, posts, and mill residue.

Printed by BoD™in Norderstedt, Germany

9 780656 860234